Clueless George Takes On Liberals!
copyright 2007 Pat Bagley

Printed in the United States

editor: Dan Thomas

First Edition

9 8 7 6 5 4 3 2 1

ISBN-10: 0-9744860-7-8
ISBN-13: 978-0-9744860-7-9

White Horse Books
1347 S. Glenmare St., Salt Lake City, UT 84105
(801) 556-4615

Special thanks to
Roger and Rob, clueless liberals.

Clueless George

Takes On LIBERALS!

Pat Bagley

White Horse Books

This is George.
George likes to dress up.
George is the president.

George is a monkey.

This is Bertrand.
Bertrand studies hard.
Bertrand cares about people.
Bertrand always plays fair.
Bertrand is a liberal.

Bertrand is a jackass.

One day Bertrand received
an invitation in the mail.

Clueless George was throwing a party!

"George is mean and stupid and conceited and he makes stuff up!" said Bertrand.

"I won't go!"

"You WILL go!" said Bertrand's mother. "George is the president. You will go and be nice and have fun. Don't spoil it! Someday, *you* might be president."

Bertrand promised his
mother he would go
and be nice
and have fun.

Ding-dong! rang the doorbell.

The Man answered the door. (George lived with The Man.)
"Oh, it's you," he said. "George! Your little
liberal friend the jackass is here!"

"The name is Bertrand, Sir," said Bertrand.

"If you say so, Jackass."

"Hey, everybody," said George, "Butt-end is here!"

The kids at the party all giggled.

Bertrand turned very red.
"George, you know my name is really Bertrand."

"What's the matter?
Can't take a joke, Butt-end?"

Bertrand remembered the promise he made to his mother to be nice.
"'Butt-end.' Ha, ha, ha!
That's a good one, George."

"What did you get me?"
asked George.

"It's a book,"
said Bertrand.

"Oh," replied George. "Well, my father's friends got me
an oil company and a baseball team and a
governorship and a . . ."

"Ahem!" said The Man.

"Anyway," said George, "I don't have time to read."

"Now we will sing a song I made up.
It goes like this . . .

"BIN LADEN AND BUTT-END,
SITTIN' IN A TREE,
K-I-S-S-I-N-G!"

Bertrand felt himself
getting angry. "I am
against terrorists!"

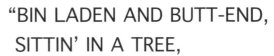

"But he didn't say he was against
kissing boys!" George helpfully
pointed out.

Bertrand was starting to get mad, but he remembered his promise.

"Now I have a special treat," said George, and a man stepped out from behind a curtain . . .

. . . KARL THE KLOWN!

"Karl is a wiz at tricks!
Karl is a wiz at games!
Karl is a wiz at rigging elec . . ."

"WONK! WONK!" interrupted Karl.

"Oh, yeah!" said George, "Karl wants Butt-end to smell his flower."

"It's called a Turd Blossom flower," said George.

"Karl, that was not nice. Shake Butt-end's hand to show there are no hard feelings."

Bertrand didn't think Karl was very funny. But he remembered his promise and didn't say anything.

"Wonk! Wonk! Wonk!" said Karl.

"Karl wants to play a new game," said George. "It is called 'Blind Man's Bluff.'"

"Bertrand will be It!"

"OUCH! OUCH! OUCH!"
Bertrand yelped.

"George, that doesn't look
funny," a girl said. "That
looks like it hurts!"

"He is a liberal and
doesn't feel pain like
the rest of us,"
explained George.
"He is like those
frogs I used to
stuff with lit fire-
crackers . . ."

"Wonk!" Karl the Klown
interrupted.

"Oh, yeah!" said George.
"It's time for another fun game!"

"I know this game!" Bertrand said.
"It's 'Bobbing for Apples.'"

"You get to go first, Butt-end," said George. "But we must tie
you up so you won't cheat."

Bertrand was appalled that anyone would think he was a
cheater. If anyone was a cheater, it wasn't him. But once
again he remembered his promise and bit his tongue.

"What is that board for?" he asked.

"Waterboarding!" George said with a cheer.

Splash! Splash! Splash! went Bertrand.

Gasp! Gasp! Gasp! gasped Bertrand.

"Butt-end, you stink at this game," said George. "Why, when I was President-in-Chief of a fraternity we would make the pledges take off all their clothes and then we would make them bend over and get a red-hot coat hanger and . . ."

"Harumph!" harumphed The Man. "It is time for the next game."

"Oh, yeah!" said George. "We will play a muscular and robust game . . .

". . . it is called 'Boxing!'"

"I will bob and weave, bob and weave," said George as he bobbed and weaved.

"You must
stand there
and take it."

"I win! I win!
I am the master of disaster!
I AM THE GREATEST!"
declared George.

"I AM THE
GREATEST!"
he added, in case
anybody had
missed it the
first time.

"Hey, George," said a boy.
"Isn't it time for dessert?"

"Here! Have some cake!"

And the boy gave George some cake.

"We're going now. We're bored."

And the girl gave George a board.

"But I am the president! I am the decider and I get to decide when you get to go and I say you can't go until I decide to say you can. I am a winner and Butt-end is a weak and whimpy loser! I am tough on terror-ists and bad guys and evil-doers and freedom-haters and everybody who is not on my side, which is the right side because I am the Commander-in-Chief of everybody who thinks rightly!"

"No, George," said the kids, "You are a jerk."

"Going somewhere?" asked The Man.

"No one walks until the monkey says so."

"Look over there! A terrorist!"

"Where?" said The Man.

"Too bad about your clown, Mr. Man."

"Wha . . . what happened?"
asked Bertrand.

"We got sick and tired of
George," said the kids.
"He is mean and stupid
and conceited and he
makes stuff up."

Bertrand thought for a
moment. "Maybe if I acted
tough and swaggered like
George, then someday I
could be president, too."

"No, Bertrand. We like it
that you study hard and
care for people and play
fair. We don't even care
that you're a liberal,
because compared to
George . . ."

". . . you're just a little jackass."

The End